THROUGH
THEIR EYES

WORDS UNLEASHED

Edited By Lynsey Evans

First published in Great Britain in 2024 by:

Young Writers
Remus House
Coltsfoot Drive
Peterborough
PE2 9BF
Telephone: 01733 890066
Website: www.youngwriters.co.uk

All Rights Reserved
Book Design by Ashley Janson
© Copyright Contributors 2024
Softback ISBN 978-1-83565-870-3
Printed and bound in the UK by BookPrintingUK
Website: www.bookprintinguk.com
YB0608L

FOREWORD

Since 1991, here at Young Writers we have celebrated the awesome power of creative writing, especially in young adults, where it can serve as a vital method of expressing strong (and sometimes difficult) emotions, a conduit to develop empathy, and a safe, non-judgemental place to explore one's own place in the world. With every poem we see the effort and thought that each pupil published in this book has put into their work and by creating this anthology we hope to encourage them further with the ultimate goal of sparking a life-long love of writing.

Through Their Eyes challenged young writers to open their minds and pen bold, powerful poems from the points-of-view of any person or concept they could imagine – from celebrities and politicians to animals and inanimate objects, or even just to give us a glimpse of the world as they experience it. The result is this fierce collection of poetry that by turns questions injustice, imagines the innermost thoughts of influential figures or simply has fun.

The nature of the topic means that contentious or controversial figures may have been chosen as the narrators, and as such some poems may contain views or thoughts that, although may represent those of the person being written about, by no means reflect the opinions or feelings of either the author or us here at Young Writers.

We encourage young writers to express themselves and address subjects that matter to them, which sometimes means writing about sensitive or difficult topics. If you have been affected by any issues raised in this book, details on where to find help can be found at
www.youngwriters.co.uk/contact-lines

CONTENTS

Durrington High School, Worthing

Leo McBean (12)	1
Grace Packer (12)	2
Hollie McCullough (12)	4
Marley Edwards (12)	5
Sophie Hopkins (12)	6
Freddie McGeorge-Hinks (13)	7

Melbury College - Lavender Campus, Mitcham

Mia Thompson (15)	8
Anna Nye (14)	10
Kianu Stander (14)	11
Iggy Rinaldi (14)	12

Newlands Girls' School, Maidenhead

Yin Lam (Erela) Fung (12)	13
Eliza George (12)	14
Edie Wespieser (12)	15
Huda Al-Jawahiri (15)	16
Layla Craig (14)	17
Alicia Delacour (12)	18

Sexey's School, Bruton

Layla Hole (15)	19
Sylva-Rose Yeoman Mills (12)	20
Lottie Sion (12)	21
Beatrice Guest (12)	22
Marcus Audley	23
Helena Marquez-Bussey (12)	24
Alwin Shaju (12) & Cece	25

The Streetly Academy, Streetly

Challie-Ray Cooper (14)	26
William Green (14)	27
Lilly-May Nolan (13)	28
Grace Kelly (12)	30
Max Openshaw (12)	31
Avani Aujla (13)	32
Poppy Thornton (14)	34
Ruby Crook (13)	35
Rowan Field (12)	36
Isabella Ellison (14)	37
Amelia Green (11)	38
Amelia Hart (12)	39
Lexie Muller (11)	40
Isobel Tack (12)	41
Holly Perks (12)	42
Zara Iqbal (14)	43
Finley Hyde (11)	44
Daisy Breakwell (14)	45
Jake Haines (13)	46
Alfie Kelly (11)	47
Lexi Short (12)	48
Isla Brabury (13)	49
Chelsie Sprague (12)	50
Skye Jones (12)	51
Aidan Keyte (11)	52
Elliott Griffiths (13)	53
Austin Pringle-Vears (13)	54
Harry Worledge (13)	55
Darcie Hale (13)	56
P Hayer (13)	57
Rio Powell (13)	58
Charlie Dyke (13)	59
Lucas Tandy (14)	60
Jess Davis (13)	61

Mia Barton (11)	62		Kayla Timms (12)	105
Ace Allen (13)	63		Rosie Case (14)	106
Amelia Hibbs (11)	64		Holly Widdowson (13)	107
Tommy McLinden (13)	65		Dylan Omer (12)	108
Chloe Perkins (13)	66		Tiannah Bambury (12)	109
Thomas Dobson (13)	67		Kara Simpson (13)	110
Megan Hawthorne (11)	68		Elena Koumides (13)	111
Jaya Bujarh (11)	69			
Eva Adly (13)	70			

Waseley Hills High School, Rubery

Violet Partridge (11)	71			
Summer Whittle (13)	72		Trixie-Ann Pullen (11)	112
Daisy-May Coyne (12)	73		Taryn Bowron (12)	114
Rosie Booker (14)	74		Holly Eastwood (13)	116
Isaac Oakes-Dennis (11)	75		Isaac Casey-Jones (13)	117
Lauren Braund (13)	76		Jess Atkinson (13)	118
Danielle Scott (13)	77		Rose Turner (12)	119
Reet Ark (12)	78		Jessica Sharp (12)	120
Harry Beesley (14)	79		Toby Ross (13)	121
Jamie Packer (13)	80		Evie Morgan (13)	122
Rowan Wilkes (12)	81		Joseph Kelly (12)	123
Zuzanna Butryn (14)	82		Ava Parton (12)	124
Ibrahim Mahmud (14)	83		Juliet Latham (13)	125
Marley Lanns (11)	84		Sophia Seymour-Twist (12)	126
Joseph Szabo (12)	85		Ruby Addis (12)	127
Lalita Kumar (12)	86		Alfred Porter (12)	128
Miriam Hoq (12)	87		Amelia Turner (13)	129
Emilee Fellows (12)	88		Pepper Pedley (12)	130
Rania Adeel (13)	89		Mirren-Rose McMillan (13)	131
Amber Partridge (14)	90		Sam Hallett (13)	132
Danny Field (14)	91		Nathaniel Matyga (12)	133
Annabelle Vigrass (13)	92		Summer Murphy (12)	134
Mary Entwistle (12)	93		Maisie-Lea Marsh (12)	135
Finn Sandland (14)	94		Julian Kaczorowski (12)	136
Xavier Painter (13)	95		Charlie Ward (12)	137
Jemima Woodhall (12)	96		Reece Roberts (12)	138
Andreas Preston (12)	97		Olivia Lowe (12)	139
Jack Palmer (13)	98		Paige Roberts (12)	140
Harper Gisborn (11)	99		Harrison Allsop (12)	141
Sam Beesley (11)	100		Winnie Day (13)	142
Nia Westaway (13)	101		Isabella Custance (13)	143
Lily-Rose Sandland (12)	102		Lola McNally (12)	144
Jaiden Palmer (14)	103		Ryan Gillam (13)	145
Liv Curtis (13)	104		Taha Kamal (13)	146
			Isla Bartlett (12)	147

Name	Number
Amelia Houghton (11)	148
Jemima Hickman-Smith (11)	149
Kacey Cleaver (12)	150
Zak Gibbons (12)	151
Aaron Codinotti (12)	152
Sebastian Haywood-Newman (13)	153
Sam McAuliffe (13)	154
Kasey Footes (12)	155
Alfie Groves (12)	156
Layla Wheeler (13)	157
Olivia-Mae Brown (11)	158
Zak Gibbons (12)	159
Kasie Rebolo (13)	160
Dylan Sherwood (12)	161
Oscar Jabbari (13)	162
Hayden Mills (12)	163
Kaitlin Prideaux (12)	164
Nicole Pinho (12)	165
Jennie-Rose Newey (12)	166
Aiden Fisher (13)	167
Bobby Barker (11)	168
Thomas Mansell (12)	169
Charlie Wall (12)	170
Maximus Ball (11)	171
Oscar Larkin (13)	172
Abigail Holden (12)	173
Lily-May Murren (13)	174
Isaac Harley (11)	175
Harrison Porter (13)	176
Charlie Such (12)	177

THE
POEMS

Nature

In forests deep, where shadows dance,
And vines whisper secrets grand,
Nature weaves its mystic trance,
In every leaf, in every strand.
The moonlight paints the silent trees,
As stars above sing ancient lore,
Its whispers concealed by the breeze,
The mysteries of nature soar.
Beneath the earth, caverns vast,
Where crystals gleam and echoes ring,
A world unseen, a timeless cast,
Where wonders hide and shadows cling,
From mountaintops to oceans deep,
Where creatures dwell in hidden grace,
In every corner, secrets keep,
A world of wonder to embrace.
So let us wonder, curious hearts,
Through valleys green and mountains high,
For the mysteries nature imparts,
We find the magic of the sky.

Leo McBean (12)
Durrington High School, Worthing

The Eagle

Up in the sky,
Where an eagle soars high,
Over Yellowstone Park, it roams.

Over the grass,
And the trees coloured brass,
Yellowstone is where it calls home.

Over the buffalo right next to the stream,
And over the geysers spitting out steam,
Dodging the water thrown into the air.

He spots some grey wolves hunting their prey,
A herd of mule deer didn't expect this today,
And yet he flies on without a care.

And into the fields where he sees some black bears,
A mother and her cubs with their spiky black hairs,
In summer, they're trying to fish.

Coyotes are next with their pointy ears,
They're munching on a kill with teeth like spears,
The eagle flies over with disgust, *what a gruesome dish!*

He soars to the mountains where another eagle rests,
She's guarding three eggs and she's doing her best,
He lands in the nest at the top of the tree.

The eggs start to crack and wiggle around,
One chick bursts out, its white feathers profound,
At Yellowstone Park, he'll always be free.

Grace Packer (12)
Durrington High School, Worthing

The Pen

Soft. The soft paper
The beautiful paper
The hope of the pen
Hoping to achieve a goal
A writer's goal.

A pen to go around the
World or not
The joy of the pen touching paper
The heartwarming writing
The glimpse of the words on
The page.

The fear of losing
Disappointment
The pen's feelings all
Go to waste
The beginning of an era
The pen has become one
With the paper
The pen is successful.

Hollie McCullough (12)
Durrington High School, Worthing

A Person's Riddle

Some people crave this
Others have it
It spreads like fire
But in the end, it's as cold as ice

When you finally find it
You treasure it and keep it safe
But not all locks are hidden

It can drive people apart
Or bring them together
Because the dove doesn't always sing
Their blissful melody

But whatever it is
At least you
Can have it.

Marley Edwards (12)
Durrington High School, Worthing

Summer's Eyes

Winter's storms, pain striking down from the skies,
To Summer's lawns, emerald lush hope and surprise,
There is Winter's cries and Summer's blue skies,
Autumn's laughs and Spring's triumphant, bold march,
But never forget Summer's optimism,
Look forward, away from the dull, grey skies,
Don't let it be a surprise,
Next time you look into Summer's eyes.

Sophie Hopkins (12)
Durrington High School, Worthing

The Bad War

The young woman buried in the city she came from.
A solitary man mourning her death on the shores of a distant country.
Far across the sea, hands raised to God's throne of despair with prayers never answered.

Freddie McGeorge-Hinks (13)
Durrington High School, Worthing

Firefighter

A cacophony of shouting
Sirens and people doubting
Swerving and speeding
While everyone else is leaving
In the distance smoke is rising
My colleagues start analysing
A crowd of wide eyes and gasps
Fire has the building in its grasp
Charging towards the action
This wasn't an overreaction
Smashing down the charred door
The fire destroying all the decor
Heart racing, adrenaline pumping
Smoke stinging, fire burning
Searching frantically everywhere
Trying not to breathe in the smog-filled air
Below the hose starts spraying
Drenching the house, but it starts swaying
Vision impaired and running out of time
I can't fail now, while someone's life is on the line
Breaking through another door
I finally find the person, but they're lying on the floor
Rushing to their side
Filled with relief that they are still alive
Speeding out of the building the air is full of alarms
Speeding out of the building with the person in my arms

The paramedics race towards me
Seeing the house topple, civilians still flee
Now everything is over
The others start to take over
I'm lost in a sea of claps
Congratulations and back-pats.

Mia Thompson (15)
Melbury College - Lavender Campus, Mitcham

The Coldness (A Soldier's Perspective)

Cold is the mud squelching up my clothes
Cold is the rain drip, drip, dripping
Cold is the can of soup I have to eat
Coldness is the lump in my throat I can never seem to swallow
Cold is the feeling of dread in my stomach
Coldness is the pounding in my head and the pang in my heart as I picture my family's faces (how long has it been?)
Coldness is longing, yearning to see their faces again
Cold is the feeling in my chest when I lose another friend
Cold is the dugout as I attempt to sleep
Coldness is what I have to carry with me or else I'll be next.
The next time I see them, will they be burying me instead?
Coldness looms. Its presence never seems to leave
Its vice-like grip tightens with every passing day
Warm is a nearby explosion
Warm is the feeling of blood gushing.
A piece of shrapnel sticking out of my skull
The coldness envelops me.

Anna Nye (14)
Melbury College - Lavender Campus, Mitcham

My Lost One (Bereavement)

I spend my day wondering if you're up there,
Running on the fluffiest clouds and drinking the fresh rainwater.

I hope you get all your favourite treats and endless cuddles from everyone up there.

I know you haven't been gone for long, but it feels like decades.

I sit by my window with tears in my eyes gazing up at the stars.

I wish you didn't have to go so soon.

I know you're somewhere up there, but I wish you could be down here with me, sitting on my bed, cuddling and falling asleep with you in my arms.

Kianu Stander (14)
Melbury College - Lavender Campus, Mitcham

I Am An Athlete
(And most of my life looks like this)

A thlete, the challenges of the mind and body
T raining, time to focus
H opeful, form is temporary
L osing, I am not perfect yet
E xhausted, it will all pay off
T ime-consuming, every minute counts
E lation, learn to love the process.

Iggy Rinaldi (14)
Melbury College - Lavender Campus, Mitcham

My Best Friends

Best friends are far,
Best friends are near,
They will be there to lend an ear,
They listen laugh and care,
But most of all they're always there,
We did everything together,
We shared every tear,
And felt each other's fear,
You all listened to everything that I said,
And never complained,
You all truly understand me,
And always knew what to say,
That's why Eliza, Pheobe, Lexie, Flossie and Immie are my best friends.

Yin Lam (Erela) Fung (12)
Newlands Girls' School, Maidenhead

Paparazzi

I walk out into the crowd
Their voices making them so loud
I can hardly hear my own thoughts
Now feeling so distraught

They bombard me with endless words
But how could I be heard
Life like this is every day
When will I escape the paparazzi?

At my concert, I try to sing
But all I can hear is the ping
Of phones and cameras around me
When will I escape the paparazzi?

Eliza George (12)
Newlands Girls' School, Maidenhead

Click, Boom, Darkness

Trussed and bound
I was taken
Lost but never found
Almost forgotten
How can I live?
In a world
But I cannot
Lost in a world of darkness and pain
Drowning, trying to escape in vain
I am trapped in a room
The door swings open
Click, boom
Pain.

Edie Wespieser (12)
Newlands Girls' School, Maidenhead

Mind

The mind is wild,
A place of clutter,
A place for growth,
An escape from reality,
A storm, fire, natural disaster,
A fiasco of clips,
An uprising of memories,
A story of life through your footsteps,
A library of thoughts,
But who would we be otherwise?

Huda Al-Jawahiri (15)
Newlands Girls' School, Maidenhead

Homosapiens

In the beginning, it was simple,
I was discovering myself,
They were too,
When they were free of ideals,
But they changed,
Consumed by fear and fate,
They were gone.

Layla Craig (14)
Newlands Girls' School, Maidenhead

The Resting Mountain
A haiku poem

In a snow blanket.
I will sleep until my time,
Unharmed by the heat.

Alicia Delacour (12)
Newlands Girls' School, Maidenhead

Wishing For A Friend

People are harsh, full of greed
They're all too selfish to think of me
Why would they? They don't care
I'm still human, but it's not fair
No one stops to listen to me plead
Can't they just help one person in need
All I ask is for one little penny
What's their problem? They've got plenty
A smile in the distance beams a glimmer of hope
Might they be the one, a chance to cope?
Step by step this all seems great
Will they help and become my best mate
They don't know how much I struggle
My whole life has been a trouble
The sound of coins ringing in my ears
A couple of drops and there goes my fears
A bit of kindness was all it took
For someone to give me a whole new look
A chance at life is what I get
Now I can live without any threat
All it took was one kind soul
Now it's your time to help us, make it your goal.

Layla Hole (15)
Sexey's School, Bruton

People Walk Past

Do you know what it's like to be homeless?
I do.
People walk past without a care,
Glancing in my direction, they look me up and down with a wide, judgemental stare.
People walk past without a care.

People walk past, disgusted by me,
They never used to be,
Now my dirty nails and scraggly hair give me away, the tramp on the street, that's all they see,
People walk past, disgusted by me.

People don't see what happens to me,
The gritty sidewalk stamped into my thigh, the cold wind I breathe into my lungs burns as I sigh,
People don't see what happens to me.

People don't see that a home makes them free,
These favoured, fortunate strangers walk away, engulfed in their own minuscule matters,
Leaving my hopeless mind in tatters.
People don't see that a home makes them free,
I do.

Sylva-Rose Yeoman Mills (12)
Sexey's School, Bruton

The Ocean Poem

I am the ocean, warm or cold at dusk or at dawn.
I provide homes to marine life.
I am beautiful but the plastic encountered causes me strife.
The animals die off so use less plastic,
And let marine life live a good life.
I am a shark, a greedy cheater and the king of the ocean.
I am a whale, I travel in slow motion.
I am gentle and not meant to be mean.
I am a big blue whale with a big blue heart.
I am a dolphin, we chitter and chirp and dance and play.
I whistle, click and squeak, so wild and free.
I am a turtle, wise and patient, every so often I pop up for a quick breath.
Then, in the blink of an eye, gone.
To travel the depths of the sea.

Lottie Sion (12)
Sexey's School, Bruton

The Wild Swimmer's Love
Inspired by Sonnet 18 by William Shakespeare

Shall I compare thee to walking along the shore?
The vast ocean waiting to be explored,
Listening to the crashing of the waves,
Beneath the expanse of the big blue swathes,
The flowing of the water has its own special peace,
The sand, the sky and the ocean blue, it's just me and you,
You are the ocean to me, the best thing to ever been,
You shan't crash and break like the waves of the ocean today,
Nor shall you be eroded or worn away like the sand today,
You shall swim wild and free day after day.
So long as people can swim and tides can change,
Your ocean-likeness shall never be erased.

Beatrice Guest (12)
Sexey's School, Bruton

World Cup-Winning Goal

In the final moments of the game, the tension was high
It was all tied when the clock began to run dry
The atmosphere was immense, their voices loud and wild
As the players battled on for that winning goal.
The ball passed with a precise point, they all worked as one
Their shots never undone.
The ball was in the air, the crowd held their breath.

The goalkeeper stretched towards the ball, stretched to save
The ball was too brave, as it flew into the net.
The World Cup-winning goal, it was all too hard to miss
What a moment of bliss.

Marcus Audley
Sexey's School, Bruton

The Foreboding Light

I am the creature that waits in the dark,
I am the one that lures them into death's ark,
I am the shadow who flits in the gloom,
I am the one that forces them into their tomb,
I am the monster that resides in the depths of the ocean,
I am the one who mixes the Reaper's potion,
I am the one who holds my lantern of pain,
I am the one that leads them down the lane,
I am the king of the deep,
Where no one dares to make a creak,
For I am the anglerfish.

Helena Marquez-Bussey (12)
Sexey's School, Bruton

Power Of Cheese Puffs

The taste of a cheese puff through and through,
Is better than an amazing view.
Without the powdered cheese, what would I do?
If I forget my beloved cheese puffs I cannot think straight,
I would be laughed at by my mate,
After failing a date.
I love my cheese puffs,
Everyone else would agree,
If I studied cheese puffs at university,
I'm sure I would get a degree.

Alwin Shaju (12) & Cece
Sexey's School, Bruton

Elon Musk And Space

In the world of innovation, time, and space,
there stands a man with a vision so brave and eligible, Elon Musk.
His name echoes far and wide all around the world.
A father, a dreamer, a thinker, with nothing to hide or lose.

A man with intelligence higher than any man there is,
Elon Musk rose to the top,
starting with nothing, working with just a laptop and some books,
a few friends, and a little bit of money.

From working at home with nothing to PayPal, Tesla, and Space X too,
pushing boundaries with no limit,
he pushes himself until failure, and breaking through walls.

A mind never rests and is always thinking ahead
Mars co-ordinator and producer, making electric cars and solar speed.
His passion inspires others to think outside the box and focus on themselves.

So here's to the man himself, Elon Musk,
a man of great might, who leads us to the future,
may his dreams inspire all who started with nothing, to think how to reach their dreams and achieve them.

Challie-Ray Cooper (14)
The Streetly Academy, Streetly

The Once Great River

A lone river stood,
Long and wide through the wood,
One significant, stopping force,
Never hidden, always perceived,
Except one day, it meant nothing, and the next it caused a stir,
Now it flows across to the city into the horizon,
The lives of those there, it does heighten,
To power machines, the ones that give life,
Also, the ones that cause strife,
Others to make clothes, and those that cause people to loathe,
At the start of every day,
The people of the town gather at the river bank to chant and say,
"River, oh river," and so it would flow,
Though rather than the cycle starting anew,
Something happened, something askew,
Rather than leaving its base,
The river retracted, into the distance,
The people, thrown into dismay,
Could not cope, for another single day,
After some time, the river returned to the town, dismal and grey,
Nobody was there, the buildings desolate, and nobody appeared, not for another single day.

William Green (14)
The Streetly Academy, Streetly

My Name Is Milo-Wren And I Really Hope We Meet Again

My lovely family,
How much I never wanted to leave you,
To stay by your side,
And to see you smile so wide.
But it was my time to leave,
I am so sorry to make you grieve.
Please don't cry,
Just wipe those tears dry.
Let's go and look back at our favourite memories,
I sure hope you never forget these...

Before you went to school I loved to play
And I really hoped it made your day.
When we went on walks I tried to be the guide,
Trotting ahead with all of my pride.
I swore to give all of you my best protection,
Although it was useless when I was given affection.
I loved to bark,
I loved to snore,
You guys swore it sounded more like a roar.
With all of this I did, I knew that you all loved me, I'm sure.

Now that all those tears have dried,
Just realise that I do appreciate how much you all tried.
I love you forever and ever,
I will forget you never.
My name is Milo-Wren,
And I really hope we meet again.

Lilly-May Nolan (13)
The Streetly Academy, Streetly

Learn To Love You

Here it is again, the sadness I fear
Which started from that one tear
But no one will know the cause
Of sitting there like you're on pause
Alone, zoned out with my thoughts
Empty with no joy because of their taunts
The feeling of being lost with no one there
But they say, "That's just fair."

I want it to stop, to just go away
But it's impossible because of what they say
Every single day, almost on loop
Commenting on me as if they can't see true beauty, that is how low they'll stoop
But no more, I'm putting them on mute and I'm going to speak up
Since I am now happy and all it took was to leave it for a while
And I got back my smile
All of this joy I feel is because of the people who are real.

No longer broken since I replaced bad and being sad with
Love for me and everyone can see
I'm happy now.

Grace Kelly (12)
The Streetly Academy, Streetly

The Blue Blanket

The ice-cold water hit me harder than a rock,
Time seemed to freeze,
Adrenaline crushed my head,
Knowing I was floating upon my deathbed,
Then the pain felt like a thousand needles,
Distracting my thoughts, blurring my vision,
Setting me adrift on the riverbed,
Where I most certainly would be dead,
There was no point fighting the river's wrath.
I surrendered to the blue blanket,
Yet through this terror,
A single ray of light shone upon me,
Encouraging me to push through,
My senses returned,
My vision was now filled with hope,
My legs felt like they were being dragged down mercilessly by a hand,
The light grew with every kick, but so did the struggle,
It illuminated the icy depths,
The surface was in sight,
I felt like a prisoner, with my body aching
Nevertheless, my head emerged with a sense of victory,
In the full moon, nobody was in sight.

Max Openshaw (12)
The Streetly Academy, Streetly

An Eagle Eye

Soaring from branch to branch,
I felt a gust of wind hit my feathers,
Soaring from branch to branch,
I could sense a child trying to chase me.

Soaring from branch to branch,
Then stop!
Suddenly I felt a shiver of pain,
I was stuck!

No more scaring,
No more hunting,
No more staring,
I was stuck!

How?
Why?
Where?
What was I going to do?

Preparing myself,
Eyes open,
Looking down at my feet,
It was a plastic bottle.

Looking out in disbelief,
Questioning what I was going to do,
It fit like a glove,
Was I just going to have to live with it?

Attempting to fly,
I was getting ready,
When suddenly,
The branch saved my life!

I could soar from branch to branch,
Get chased,
Feel my feathers,
I was free again!

Avani Aujla (13)
The Streetly Academy, Streetly

Through The Eyes Of The Sun

I sit here, watching and waiting,
"Waiting for what?" you ask me,
For I am the sun, there is no debating,
And there is nothing I don't see.

I see these objects floating in the empty sky,
I wonder if they feel anything at all,
Big metal machines that come and pass me by,
Flying and floating around me, why don't they fall?

The live forms on Earth, move and live,
What they do, I don't know,
Every year when I hide away, it is a time to give,
This white stuff covers countries, I think it's called snow.

It makes me sad to think there is no one for me,
I see other planets with moons that orbit around them,
I suppose I'll wait another 4.6 billion years and see,
I want - no, need - a moon like a plant needs a stem.

Poppy Thornton (14)
The Streetly Academy, Streetly

Refugee Life

The war started
Crash! Bang! Boom!
I heard these noises from my room
The enemy had finally come
I screamed, terrified for my mum
I packed some clothes and ran out the door
Emptying my chest of drawers
I found my mum; we needed to flee
Luckily, we lived near the sea
We got on a boat to a foreign place
Everyone was running, like in a race
I was terrified to leave my home
I was scared to be all alone
My mum was silent, fearing for her life
Before we realised someone had a knife
We tried to stay calm but jumped off the boat
I was panicking; I couldn't stay afloat
I watched my mum as she slowly died
She closed her eyes while I cried
At last, I was the final one
Until I finally decided I was done.

Ruby Crook (13)
The Streetly Academy, Streetly

Where Did It All Go?

I remember when I was a chick - still hiding between my parents.
My fluffy grey feathers rustling in the Antarctic wind.
But I'll never forget the day it all came crashing.
The fluffy white snow shook as big machinery on trailers rolled in.
Big, tall giants wearing puffy tomato coats clipped my wing - I couldn't fly anyway.
I cried aloud for help as the heat rose.
Where was everybody? Was I the only one who didn't want this?
My cousins, brothers and aunts walked and waddled, so nonchalantly, did they know?
I called for help.
The tomato men said I'd be gone by 2100.
But what if I didn't want to be?
I, a single, flightless bird, cannot make the change, but you, you can.
So I ask this final question. Where did it all go?

Rowan Field (12)
The Streetly Academy, Streetly

Through The Eyes Of A Willow Tree

I stood upon my hill,
My roots dug deep into the ground,
The wind was gentle and chill,
As two lovers sat upon my mound,
Their love was etched into my bark,
Their art outlined with a love heart.

Over the years I stood on the hill,
The bright sun had grown dark.
The dim light stood still,
Dull and grey upon my hill.
The two lovers no longer talked,
Their love slowly becoming nought.
Their love that was once etched with chalk,
May not last as long as I thought.

I stand weak upon my hill,
My leaves withered and the sky covered in grey.
The once clean ground now resembling a landfill,
The two lovers have grown apart since that day.
That day they met, seated upon my hill.

Isabella Ellison (14)
The Streetly Academy, Streetly

Save Them Now

I never knew much about our waters.
Waves just splashed and danced about.
Little did I know that there was so much more.
Ten years old; and had seen dead fish and sea creatures,
Washed upon the scorching hot sand, with plastic and glass.
A single person walked past and left their rubbish near the grey, sharp rocks.
That's it! That's when I realised, one arrogant, unthoughtful person,
That has just one bad action, can affect over five sea creatures.
Turtles die every day from plastic bags they once thought were jellyfish.
Fish get caught in cans.
Think more. Speak up. And help our ocean.
Recycle and use less water when possible.
Help our oceans and world, always.
Save them now!

Amelia Green (11)
The Streetly Academy, Streetly

A Refugee

Nowhere to go, nowhere to be seen,
Nowhere meant for them, that's me,
At eight years old, the sound of war began,
Father and brother left to fight,
Whilst Mother and I ran,
We got on a boat, leaving behind everything we knew,
Mother said, "It'll be okay,"
But I didn't think that was true,
Packed like sardines in the middle of the ocean,
Fear surrounded me in a tide of emotion,
After days that felt like years, my eyes saw the land,
As I took my first step onto this foreign shore,
I longed for my father, I longed for my brother,
I longed for the face I used to see on my mother,
Nowhere to go, nowhere to be seen,
Nowhere meant for them, that's me.

Amelia Hart (12)
The Streetly Academy, Streetly

Life As A Dog

I catch a tennis ball,
Or eat a treat, chase my neighbour's annoying cat,
I love to stretch and yawn,
But one thing I hate is being alone,
Why do my family go out?
Where do they go?
As a dog, I want to curl up,
But I have to keep finding my bed,
I can cuddle up to my owners,
When they are home,
And beg for treats,
And get attention,
I can fall asleep with no sound,
But wish I could see more colours,
I can run wild in the garden,
Catch loads of leaves,
Hide in the bushes,
I've run inside and muddied the floor,
I get told off for chewing my brother's shoes,
I stand in front with my lead,
My parents give in and then take me out, yay!

Lexie Muller (11)
The Streetly Academy, Streetly

A Teddy Bear's POV

I rest my head on the pillowcase of my darling Dottie's bed.
I wait, wait so patiently for her arrival.

She comes into the room, teary-eyed, eyes red and puffy.
You can tell she's cried.
As hard as I tried, I couldn't remind her it was okay.
She put me in her sorrowed arms and held me dearly.
She knew she was loved, oh so clearly.
But to this day, I'll never know how to show my feelings.

Through my button eyes, I spectate a world where I can't relate to how she lives and how she thinks,
Because it's not what I was made for.
My fuzzy arms are too short to hug her, but my heart is large enough to love her,
My darling, precious Dottie.

Isobel Tack (12)
The Streetly Academy, Streetly

Left Behind

I go to see them,
"Oh, you're just a germ!"
That's what they say,
Almost, like every day.

Even though they leave me,
Oh, I wish they would hurry,
Even though I get told to shush,
I love them so much!

Yay! They're back,
Oh, they have a cat,
This is suspicious,
The cat looks vicious.

Ooh, yay, we're going in the car,
Wait, we're going far too far,
They opened my door,
And put me on the floor.

But they're driving away,
Wait they're not here to stay?
But I'm all alone,
Now I'm on my own.

Solo, solo, solo,
I'm feeling so low.

Holly Perks (12)
The Streetly Academy, Streetly

The Man With The Gun

Bombs plummet through the air.
In our hearts there's much despair...
Bloodshed engulfs us all.
a constant reminder that we're at war.
Casualties, combat, contention and conflict.
All of this a part of the pain they inflict.

Stop!
Quick!
Run!
There's a man coming at us with a gun.
Quick!
Run!
Hide inside!
All of a sudden there's a sharp pain down my side.
Blood pours, I've seen this before.

Bombs plummet through the air.
In my heart there was once despair.
I tried to run from the man with the gun,
But he shot me and now my life is completely done.

Zara Iqbal (14)
The Streetly Academy, Streetly

The Fake Kindness

Since the start of humanity, kindness has been everywhere
But some people think it's not the same anymore in 2024
Because people are complaining over the smallest thing
On social media
The main example is Twitter/X
Someone posts a tweet
And then someone disagrees with it
And then it goes into a full argument
I'm mainly pointing out Twitter
Because it has the most toxicity (in my opinion)
But it's not just social media
It's real life too
In school, it's more likely you'll get bullied if you have glasses
But the internet is a place for creative art
And to show a bit of our lives
And not for toxicity.

Finley Hyde (11)
The Streetly Academy, Streetly

Am I Just A Mistake?

Crawling around, trying to hide,
Hearing the cheering, thinking I died,
Why, oh why am I such a fright,
Do they really think that I bite?

I'm just a creature,
Not that hairy,
How do I seem so scary?

Listening to the sighs of relief,
While I roam in a place,
To build my new home,
In a place unknown,
All alone!

I'm just a creature,
Ever so small,
Spending my life hiding from you all.

Building after building,
To hear another scream,
Sometimes I think,
Surely it's a dream,
Here we go again,
I never get a break,
Am I just a mistake?

Daisy Breakwell (14)
The Streetly Academy, Streetly

What More Could You Ask For?

Earth is beautiful. Seven seas, seven continents,
What more could you ask for?
Beautiful animals, beautiful plants and beautiful people,
What more could you ask for?
The best tree is a beech, with branches so high, way out of reach.
When it hits fall, the leaves fall and make it look treeless, until spring comes.
The best animal is a penguin. They slip, slide and glide on the ice with not a care in life.
What more could you ask for?
Life is beautiful, so take in the moments before they go.
Yes, look at that tree swinging to and fro.
Yes, look at that penguin gliding and thriving.
It's all about moments.

Jake Haines (13)
The Streetly Academy, Streetly

Don't Wish For Everything

I'm just a kid in a class,
Confused, stuck and with no help,
All I want is a little help.
I wish I never felt like this.
I wish I didn't feel like this.
All I wish is for me never to wish again.

I wish this would all just go away,
Why me?
I never wished for this.
I wish for it all to just go away!

I wish I could go to space,
I wish I could fly,
I wish I was the smartest in my class.
I'm just a normal human,
Like everyone else who has wishes and dreams.
I wish for it all to just go away!

Why me?
What did I do?
Who did this to me?

Alfie Kelly (11)
The Streetly Academy, Streetly

I'm The Demon In The Corner

Though I might seem scary,
I'm always wary.
Some say I'm hairy,
While I say I'm creepy.

When you become sleepy,
I hop into your dreams.
While some try to possess,
I protect.

Some say I'm the odd one out,
So I give them a pout.
While you might see me and fear,
I'll come and cheer.

So now you know me as the demon in your corner.
Yet I would like to be a friend,
I have to say it depends,
As you have to beware.

Though I don't bite,
I will give you a fright.
So this is the end,
Of the demon in your corner.

Lexi Short (12)
The Streetly Academy, Streetly

Your Last Minutes

I ran for my life as I was chased through the park
He had a weapon, the sky went dark
What would happen if he ever caught me?
At that point I would never be free
Were these my last moments? Was I going to die?
This was it and I wanted to cry
No it's not, this can't be the end
I can't stay optimistic, death is my friend
I don't know this man, how dare he try and take my life
My end will be because of a knife
My heart was racing a million miles per hour
I felt like I had no power
He had caught up, I had fallen for his scheme
Then I woke up, it was all a dream.

Isla Brabury (13)
The Streetly Academy, Streetly

A Gymnast's Comp

I was standing there
By the door
Getting ready with my team
I could feel the pressure of the comp
As I put my hair up in a bun
We did the warm-up
For half an hour
Handstands and lunges
Bridges and walkovers
Now I didn't feel so worried.

The crowd was cheering
Oh so loud
There were so many people
Watching now
This was the start of the comp
Bar, beam and vault
I had already done
Just floor to do
And then I was done
Flips and cartwheels
Walkovers and handsprings
Now the comp was over.

Chelsie Sprague (12)
The Streetly Academy, Streetly

Why Does The Sky Cry?

I was in the field because I ran away from home.
I wanted to feel in a zone, as I wasn't happy at home.
When all of a sudden the clouds started to cry.

I look up at the grey, cloudy sky and wonder,
Why do the clouds cry?
Do they cry because they are happy?
Do they cry because they are sad?
Do they cry because they are angry?
Or do they cry because they are mad?

It was bright and the sky was blue,
But now that isn't true.
The sky changed from bright to dark,
And I never knew why,
The clouds started crying.

Skye Jones (12)
The Streetly Academy, Streetly

The Last Thing I Remember

The last thing I remember
Me crying in your arms
The last thing I remember
The smuggler shouting, "Come on."
The last thing I remember
Me getting on the train
I saw you tearing up
As I said goodbye again
I sat in my seat
And my heart started to beat
but...
The last thing I remember
I saw a big thing in the sky
The last thing I remember
It flying sky high
The last thing I remember
Everyone started screaming
But I started dreaming
I heard a big explosion
It felt like slow motion.

Aidan Keyte (11)
The Streetly Academy, Streetly

Nature's Peace

Strolling through the depths of the rainforest,
Listening to the rainforest's songs,
Walking through nature's finest sights,
Watching the river cover the finest rocks,
Making sounds of peace.

The birds chirped, pulling me closer,
To an animal's perfect habitat.
Whistling in sync with the river's rush,
In the heart of the rainforest's peace.

Giving off therapy to all the senses,
The rainforest in its depths,
Soothing my worst worries,
The calming rainforest,
Brings nature's peace.

Elliott Griffiths (13)
The Streetly Academy, Streetly

The Future

Deep into time, there is a place where buildings tower into the sky and cars fly.
A place of war against robots left thousands unalive.
Climate change left the planet a massive ocean and more frozen than the Arctic.
Forests were ignited and bushes were red.
The sun had died and gone black, making the moon go into a permanent eclipse.
This all meant we either had to build up to the sky or down in the ground.
Both societies were separated.
Some say they will never see each other again.
No one knows if this is the end.
Hope is all we have.

Austin Pringle-Vears (13)
The Streetly Academy, Streetly

The Last Streetlight

Abandoned,
That is what I am,
That is because of man,
I am the city's last light,
I am the sole survivor of this fight,
The conflict was an arms race,
The conflict broke this place.

Life was full of happy weeks,
Life was full of untouched peace,
I watched the people walk on by,
I watched the planes overhead fly,
One day the tanks rolled in,
One day later they would win.

Now I am alone out here,
Now I only feel fear,
I am the last streetlight,
Alone in this city of fright.

Harry Worledge (13)
The Streetly Academy, Streetly

Untitled

Love can sting like a bee
But it's sweet, like candy

Everybody craves attention and love
Till someone makes you feel unworthy and tough

Love comes with tears and fears
You want cute dates on piers until it premieres

Sometimes a heart can sink like a stone
Until you find home

You feel lonely and unknown
Till somebody makes you feel shown

Never-ending hugs and wishes
You want to be a Mr and Mrs

Love can sting like a bee
But it's sweet, like candy.

Darcie Hale (13)
The Streetly Academy, Streetly

Rashford's Return

Marcus has not being doing good in training,
This could be where he starts fading,
A good performance in the Cup,
Could guarantee his stay in the club,
Training every day,
Means there's still hope in May,
A little bit of luck,
Could help win the Cup.
Getting on the score sheet,
Could help re-find his feet.
If they get beat,
It will not look very neat.
A win will get him more confident,
And finally get some acknowledgement.
Training every day,
Means there's still hope in May.

P Hayer (13)
The Streetly Academy, Streetly

The Guest

I was made... no freedom
Kept from the rest... I haven't been used in so long
They moved on, made something new
Before I was... better... used... but
Now, I'm free, I was being used
I was put in different games
I was dragged and driven high
Thrown and even killed
I would die, die, die
And it would not end
It was torture
It was pain
I was wounded
I thought being left was good
But...
I'm just alone
Watching others
Suffer, pray, die and cry
This is Roblox.

Rio Powell (13)
The Streetly Academy, Streetly

Demons

He follows me down the dark streets of my mind,
I can hear his footsteps, following close behind,
He plays with my head,
Lives in my dreams,
He calls out to me,
Tries to lure me away,
I can't cope, so I run away,
He's still right behind me,
I just want to be free,
So please help me,
He consumes my thoughts,
I let out a cry,
But no one bats an eye,
I'm all alone,
He's given me a phone,
Everyone around has anxiety,
And then I realise,
This is just society.

Charlie Dyke (13)
The Streetly Academy, Streetly

Through The Eyes Of A Scared Soldier

In the eyes of a soldier, the world unfolds
Stories of braveness untold
Chaos and the strife
Navigating the battlefield with their life.

Eyes blurred from sleepless nights
The weight on their shoulders from the deathless fights
The horrors that no one else could bear
But they stand strong without a care.

Fighting for the freedom of our tomorrow
Through all the pain, but they can't even express sorrow
The brotherhood bond is so strong
Even through war, they will still sing a song.

Lucas Tandy (14)
The Streetly Academy, Streetly

Home

The dark nights, sitting alone,
Wondering, what is home?
As the raindrops trickle,
Down the cold window,
I wonder, what is home?
The streetlights shine and glisten,
While I wonder, what is home?

I sit there, listening to the clock,
Tick, tick, tick and I finally get it,
Home isn't just a place,
It can be a person.
A person you care so deeply for,
A person who you would do anything for,
A person who is always there,
No matter what,
What is home?
My best friend.

Jess Davis (13)
The Streetly Academy, Streetly

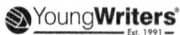

Drop The Vape And You'll Escape

Stop,
Think,
Cola, watermelon, strawberry,
Are we talking about ice lollies?
Or are we talking about inhaling chemicals?
What has our world come to?
Cameras are being put into school toilets,
No one is trusted not to be puffing on flavoured air,
The most innocent of people can try to fall into the crowd,
Don't be infuriated,
Be your own person,
Vaping will be the death of me,
Not just me,
But the thirty million people across the world too,
Drop a vape and you'll escape.

Mia Barton (11)
The Streetly Academy, Streetly

Teenage Troubles

A heart so true,
Every day is new,
So many dreams to see,
Imagine what you want to be.

Us teenagers get confused,
On what to do,
Who do we believe,
Our parents or beloved friends?

Always in two minds,
Task on mind or not,
Never get to see the positive side,
With the results we've got.

We always do what the heart says,
Paying nothing to our family,
And this is how we complete,
This tough and uneven journey.

Teenage troubles.

Ace Allen (13)
The Streetly Academy, Streetly

My Beautiful Ocean

Oh, sweet ocean, how blue you are getting.
Your turtles have to hide in tunnels,
Away from the killing circles.

Oh, sweet ocean, your coral is dying
Because those stupid humans keep doing the ironing!

Oh, sweet ocean, the stress you are under,
Yet, you are too busy fighting to have a big slumber.

Oh, sweet ocean, you have no visible sand left,
As those monsters are tossing their rubbish as a test.

Oh, sweet ocean, soon they shall see
What the Earth will be.

Amelia Hibbs (11)
The Streetly Academy, Streetly

Star Dreams

We cherish many dreams
In mind and in body
Much pleasure dreams give
Great dreams make a great believer

Dream big,
The bigger your dream,
The bigger you achieve
The more you believe
The bigger you leap to your destiny

Hold on to the dreams,
For without dreams
The world will crumble
And the stars will be crushed

Dream for the stars
And you'll reach afar.
A big dream isn't too far
In a few years
You'll be a superstar.

Tommy McLinden (13)
The Streetly Academy, Streetly

Victim

Stuck in the shop,
Held hostage,
You could even hear a pin drop,
I want to go back to my cottage.

A gun held up to my head,
I just want to go back to my bed.
Told to empty the till,
"Is your name Bill?"

No, I am the victim,
I will put you in the bin,
I cried,
My nan's hair is dyed.

I watch everyone get shot,
My dad was stuck in a plant pot.
My mum ran freely,
Until a bird came past and picked her up.
She was screaming.

Chloe Perkins (13)
The Streetly Academy, Streetly

Dystopia

Thirty years in the future, when smoke covers the sky,
climate change has ruined Earth and many things will die.
Flying cars go around and footballers don't leave the ground
the sea has turned black and now there is no way of going back
I miss when the park was green, and when the sky was blue
but now I can't even buy a shoe.
The cost of living has gone up a lot,
and now everyone has lost the plot.
This was my poem about the future,
now be careful what you put on your computer.

Thomas Dobson (13)
The Streetly Academy, Streetly

Forest Years

F rom all the years I have been here
O nly I have seen such things
R oaming dinosaurs had me in fear
E very leaf that came
S till holds each memory the same
T hrough rough storms and blazing sunlight

Y et the seasons are changing and it's becoming so bright
E ndless summers are my favourite time
A nd all us trees are doing just fine
R ooted deep, my branches so wide
S everal years with nature by my side.

Megan Hawthorne (11)
The Streetly Academy, Streetly

It's All Going To Be Okay

I had a grandma,
Who lived in Canada.
We saw her for my birthday,
And that was the best.
It's all going to be okay.
She got breast cancer,
And luckily survived.
The chemo gave her blood cancer,
She spent loads of time in hospital.

I came home from school,
And the house was quiet.
My mom was in Canada
To be with her mom
My dad sat me down,
And she was gone.
It's all going to be alright.

Now she watches down on me from the stars.

Jaya Bujarh (11)
The Streetly Academy, Streetly

Summer In The Sea

I, a youthful dolphin, awoke from my sleep,
I heard my sister trying to creep.
I swam off with a smile,
And noticed something after a mile.

It was sunny,
I got a blissful feeling in my tummy.
I jumped out of the gorgeous water,
And spotted my friend, Otter.

It was a beautiful day,
A great day to play.
The sky was bright blue,
And no one had the flu!

I heard the birds sing,
And I saw my sibling.
I love my life,
So appreciate yours.

Eva Adly (13)
The Streetly Academy, Streetly

Little Girl Standing There

Little girl standing there,
Playing in the park,
Swinging on the swings,
All until dark.

Little girl standing there,
What is the world like?
Fun, cheer and happiness,
As she rides along on her bike.

Little girl standing there,
Twirling with her hair,
Singing with no care,
Dreaming dreams of a life so fair.

Little girl standing there,
Is that a rain cloud you can see?
She starts to dance in the rain,
As free as a buzzy bumblebee.

Violet Partridge (11)
The Streetly Academy, Streetly

Be Your Own Hero!

No matter the darkness, you will find the light
I know you'll get through
I know it hurts when you are blue
It's not nice to be sad
Let's find a moment to make someone glad
Get out of the black hole and take control
Face your fear to keep your mind clear
Just take care of yourself
And take care of your health
Be strong in each hour
And be proud of your power
Always be strong
And you'll never go wrong
Be you, be true
Be your own hero!

Summer Whittle (13)
The Streetly Academy, Streetly

The Accident

I was riding on my scooter, just going down the road,
I was listening to music, not too far from home,
I came to some traffic lights, they told me to go,
But a car ran into me, oh no.
I was rushed into hospital, now so far from home,
I was fighting for my life, just trying to survive,
With swelling to my brain and staples in my head,
With a fractured collarbone and a broken leg.
No one came to visit me, I was left all alone,
Lying in a hospital bed, with nowhere to go.

Daisy-May Coyne (12)
The Streetly Academy, Streetly

Believe Me

I wish you had believed me when I told you love wasn't easy.
I wish you'd accepted the awes as well as the flaws.
Wrong people can destroy you.
The right person will love you for you.
It will be a difficult process but patience is key.
Because in the end you'll be filled with glee.

Sometimes independence is better if you're not feeling any better.
Loving someone who isn't ready will upset you.
But when it's done right it'll bless you.

Rosie Booker (14)
The Streetly Academy, Streetly

Football Is Life

F ailure, a name you can be called that can hurt you
O bnoxious after winning or losing a match
O n the ball always
T eamwork makes the dream work
B eautiful game
A ngry when you concede
L ashing out at the ref when he gives you a red card
L oving your teammates like they are your family
E motional when you win a final
R emember to never give up on your dreams and to believe in yourself!

Isaac Oakes-Dennis (11)
The Streetly Academy, Streetly

The Sky

The sky, I admire it.
I love the tranquil winds,
the glimmer of the sun in the daylight,
the white glow of the moon in the night,
the fluorescent stars, the fuzzy clouds,
and the radiant beams of light.

The sky, I admire it.
The sound of the leaves rustling,
the sound of the birds chirping and whistling,
the sound of peace.

The sky, I admire it.
I adore it, I look up to it, I cherish it.
The sky is my desire.

Lauren Braund (13)
The Streetly Academy, Streetly

The Other Side

Life on the other side.
Everyone else had a great time,
But on this side, no one had a 'great time'.
Criminals, monsters, all the same,
But on the other side, this seemed insane.
Life on the other side.

Everybody seemed joyful,
Whereas here, everyone was dismal.
I wish I could be on the other side.
Life on the other side.

Admirable.
Desirable.
Wanted.
Needed.
But you just can't grasp...

Danielle Scott (13)
The Streetly Academy, Streetly

The Forest Fire

Bright hot flames flicker,
The fire burns yet again,
A forest slowly dies,
Animals run and flee for their lives.

Men try to protect their homes,
A place so unknown,
Looking through the glass,
It is as if I'm there.

I smell and taste the smoke in the air,
Blackened skies billow above the sunrise,
Water pours from hoses for so long.

For if only they can get control of it,
Before it's all gone.

Reet Ark (12)
The Streetly Academy, Streetly

The Pencil

Began with no purpose.
Then I became precious.
However, it all fades away,
Slowly and slowly after more use.

Now back to precious next day,
Does this seem like abuse?
Adrift, astray, I am off course, off track,
Hiding away, ready to get attacked.

Forsaken and debarred I feel futile,
All of my thoughts you need to compile.
I don't want this for you, it brings me dread.
It could be possible that I am dead.

Harry Beesley (14)
The Streetly Academy, Streetly

Upcoming Superstar

Beep, beep, it's time to wake up,
It's your big day,
Mum, there's still one hour until I play,
Oh son, I'm just so excited to see my only son play,
For a youth football team, for England,
My heart skips a beat,
Hearing those words,
So nervous,
My mum was putting my kit out, ready,
I was training, getting ready,
That hour went like a second,
It was time,
My mum drove me to the airport...

Jamie Packer (13)
The Streetly Academy, Streetly

Flower Vase

F eeling helpless, I cannot move
L ooking at everyone walk past me
O verlooking me like I am nothing
W ondering when anyone will notice me
E very day
R aging with anger - wait, what if I walk or talk?

V aguely realising I will never be noticed
A nd all of a sudden
S omeone has noticed me
E very day, she brings me flowers.

I am a flower vase.

Rowan Wilkes (12)
The Streetly Academy, Streetly

Through The Eyes Of A Pen

Shame
That's what I feel
Shame that all my appeal
Is being someone else's idea

Pain
That's what I feel
Being pressed onto nature's discard
Being a disregard for others

Horror
That's what I feel
Is this all I'm destined to be
A vein of other people's hope?

Useless
That's how I feel
Always stood, always used
But never valued.

Zuzanna Butryn (14)
The Streetly Academy, Streetly

Marcus Rashford

M ost amazing skills that he wants to use to pay the bills.
A wesome teamwork from Rashford and United.
R emember that you're the greatest player for United to make us win all matches in the Premier League.
C reates emotions and works hard.
U nites the team with great goals.
S hows a respectful attitude.

R espects the manager of the team. Absolutely brilliant stuff.

Ibrahim Mahmud (14)
The Streetly Academy, Streetly

Untitled

He started off in 2004
Captaining the club
Talking, playing and being positive
Just as he should.
He joined the senior team in 2016
Swinging balls across the field
He had a few injuries in his time
but he always healed.
He played in two Champions Leagues
He won one
And lost one
At the age of eighteen.
Since the academy
He wore 66
And to this day
He still wears it.

Marley Lanns (11)
The Streetly Academy, Streetly

The Life Of A Refugee

R un! Run! Run!
E scape from death, hunger and war!
F ind a new life on Planet Earth
U nder the scorching sun, over high walls and barbed wire
G o over the hills, mountains and seas!
E nter into closed borders by foot or fragile boat
E ncounter the rejection or generosity of your hosts
S ecurity and peace that you and all others deserve!

Joseph Szabo (12)
The Streetly Academy, Streetly

Ocean Falls

Leave me alone, please
I don't do any wrong
All I do is stand strong.

You throw litter in me
And you see
All the plastic lies on me.

People, people, can you hear me?
I produce oxygen for you
And this is what I renew.

Here I am trying to flee
Whilst your cans of Coke are stopping me.

Me dying on this day
I swear you will pay.

Lalita Kumar (12)
The Streetly Academy, Streetly

Noticing Nature

Adapting, changing, hoping for the better,
We need to help, sooner than later.
We see the beauty but move past danger,
Or let nature become a stranger.

The fragile leaves and silky petals,
Can be destroyed by burning metals.
Lucious forests and open fields,
Appear so lovely but need a shield.
To protect themselves from pollution,
As that is their only solution...

Miriam Hoq (12)
The Streetly Academy, Streetly

Used Ribbon

I'm wrapped around presents,
I'm wrapped around hair,
I'm wrapped around clothes,
I'm wrapped around everywhere.

You use me for special occasions,
You use me all around,
You tie me up, and then cut me down.

But when I am gone,
Your presents won't be the same
As they were last Christmas Day.

Emilee Fellows (12)
The Streetly Academy, Streetly

Beauty Of Nature

The breeze blows as hard as it can
The wind blows as softly as it can
The grass rustles as slow as it can
And the trees sway left and right
This is the beauty of nature.

The fruits ripen and fall
The flowers bloom
Swaying with their beautiful scent
Butterflies are seen, bees heard
Nothing can be compared
To the beauty of nature.

Rania Adeel (13)
The Streetly Academy, Streetly

Footprints

Burning rays of orange
Fill the morning sky
A fireball of amber
Slowly begins to rise.

The gleaming waves retreat
Exposing golden shores
Rich with nature's treasures
Risen from the ocean floor.

A fresh salt breeze
Fires from each breaking wave
Over untrodden sands
Awaiting the first footprints of the day.

Amber Partridge (14)
The Streetly Academy, Streetly

The Last Drop

I'm everywhere yet I'm running out
I'm vital for life but I kill you,
I can be clean but polluted,
When I'm too much it's an issue,
When I'm too little it's an issue,
You can only use a fraction of me,
Yet... you waste me!
You need to save me,
I won't be around for much longer.
Sincerely,
Water.

Danny Field (14)
The Streetly Academy, Streetly

Facing The Forest Fire

The fire was wild
The ash was piled
The animals ran at great pace
As if it were a race
As the fire got more red
It started to spread
It raised higher and higher
The flames flew
The flames spun in the wind
The animals whined
They ran with fear
The fire was here
It was catching up with them
It was here again.

Annabelle Vigrass (13)
The Streetly Academy, Streetly

I Wish I Was A Fly

I wish I was a fly
And every day I cry
About not being a fly

I wish I was a fly
Because then I'd be a spy

I wish I was a fly
Although I might die
He could have been a mean guy
Or he's probably jealous that he is not a fly

Although I don't want to die
So maybe I shouldn't be a fly.

Mary Entwistle (12)
The Streetly Academy, Streetly

The Dog's Tail

I wander around
I sleep in the warmth
I wait for them to come around
And when I go forth
I hear a sound
When the door unlocks
And they come in the house
I sit there and stop
And I open my mouth
They are back home
They know I am loyal
That's why they treat me like a royal.

Finn Sandland (14)
The Streetly Academy, Streetly

I Am Ready To Rumble

I was in the changing room
I heard a boom
My heart skipped a beat
My gloves were on, I was ready to pound
I walked out and started the round
It was me, Muhammad Ali
I felt proud
When I heard the crowd
I threw a 1, 2, they started to cheer
Then I realised, the title was near.

Xavier Painter (13)
The Streetly Academy, Streetly

A Day In The Life Of My Cat

She eats all the bugs,
She wees on the rugs,
She doesn't like pugs.

She knocks on the door
When she wants to come in,
Then searches the bin.

She eats all the food,
Then brightens our mood,
Though she is always rude,
She cheers up the room.

Jemima Woodhall (12)
The Streetly Academy, Streetly

Life Of A Footballer

What is this game?
You have your ups and downs,
What is this ball?
This means the world to me,
It's all about the winning.
But even when you lose,
You still walk tall.
Our match is won,
Any crosses, any shots,
You will simply stop the lot.
Our team, your ball.

Andreas Preston (12)
The Streetly Academy, Streetly

Refugees

Last year, the man you see was not a refugee
Living his life free, little did he know he would have to travel across the sea
He had to flee because the army was on duty
I feel bad for the man
They should have let him be
But the new country was safe and that was a guarantee.

Jack Palmer (13)
The Streetly Academy, Streetly

The Death Of Me

Running through the forest
I start to scream
As the fire encloses me
I see the fear in my family's eyes
As they see the end of me
I struggle to breathe
As my body starts to ache
My brain is closing down
The pain is killing me
Is this the end of me?

Harper Gisborn (11)
The Streetly Academy, Streetly

This Is Wrong

All the prejudice
This is wrong
Like everyone is my nemesis
This is wrong
I don't feel I'm home.

All is wrong
Race takes hold
All is wrong
Like I'm controlled
All is wrong
Apart from one thing
That we can feel the sting.

Sam Beesley (11)
The Streetly Academy, Streetly

Facing The Forest Fire

The bonfire is alive,
Rising higher and higher into the sky,
The flames grew,
The animals and their children ran through,
Scared for their lives,
The world full of strife,
This is a scary place,
All the animals running,
Like it's a race.

Nia Westaway (13)
The Streetly Academy, Streetly

Why Am I Feared?

Why me?
Why am I the one you fear?
Why not fish?
Why not dolphins?
Why me?
You kill more of me than I do you
So why me?
I'm not vicious
I don't like blood
Why me?
Why am I feared
Why not fish?
Why not dolphins?

Lily-Rose Sandland (12)
The Streetly Academy, Streetly

Footballer

I came to a team called Aston Villa to start my football career,
to be the best footballer by training, getting trophies and winning the Ballon d'Or.
I want to help my team win the Premier League,
make it to the Champions League and win that trophy too.

Jaiden Palmer (14)
The Streetly Academy, Streetly

My Football Dream

In my dream, I play football but I never win and never lose
It's all a dream
But one day I'll get the courage to play
So I train and I train and I train
Through hail, sun and rain
One day I'll do it
I'll make it to the top.

Liv Curtis (13)
The Streetly Academy, Streetly

Soldiers Marching

S ave people's lives,
O ver the land,
L ooking for enemies,
D ead people on the ground,
I shoot the enemies until they die,
E veryone's lives are important,
R un away! Be strong and brave.

Kayla Timms (12)
The Streetly Academy, Streetly

The Day Of The Shooting

D eath is just another stage in life
E very life should be remembered
A t first, it seemed like a normal school day
T hen came the gunshots
H ell broke loose in the classroom when I was shot saving my sister.

Rosie Case (14)
The Streetly Academy, Streetly

Poor Dog

There, deep in the forest, I was lying,
Awaiting for my family to return.
Just a poor dog, feeling isolated and deserted,
Not long later, I was suddenly alerted,
A desperate, injured man crossed my path.

Holly Widdowson (13)
The Streetly Academy, Streetly

That Shameful Space

Remorseless murderer
Human slayer
Regretful action
Shameful gesture
Dishonourable act
Freezing space
I'm displaced
Sorrowful face
I'm a prisoner in an unhappy place.

Dylan Omer (12)
The Streetly Academy, Streetly

The Truthful Leaf

There was one isolated leaf
One-of-a-kind leaf
It had feelings, sometimes sad,
Sometimes happy
Sometimes it got stomped on
And was not very happy
As it got left alone, it got sad.

Tiannah Bambury (12)
The Streetly Academy, Streetly

Who Am I?

Never calm
Always rowing
Jumping playfully
Snoring violently
Playful like a puppy
Razor-sharp teeth always snapping
Active spirit
People pushover
I am Kiio the dog!

Kara Simpson (13)
The Streetly Academy, Streetly

My Mother
A kennings poem

Memory maker
Worry eraser
Professional baker
Patient waiter
She is my mother.

Elena Koumides (13)
The Streetly Academy, Streetly

Detentions

Wake her up,
She turns off my alarm.
She texts her crush, she starts to laugh,
Her mum tells her to "*Shush.*"

She gets ready, puts her lunch money in her bag,
Then calls her dad.
"Miles, the keys are down here,
Why are they in a rag?"

Her bag, in I go,
First, on 'silent'.
I get used in maths,
I get taken off her.
Whoops,
Now everybody laughs.

She gets lunch detention,
And I get sent to reception.
Mmmm, there's nothing to do here,
A new face I've not seen before.

Three hours go by,
The student receptionists talk to her.
Whoops, wrong classroom,
The English block.

There, she is yelling, "Sir!"
I'm back with Miles, and now she smiles.

Trixie-Ann Pullen (11)
Waseley Hills High School, Rubery

Mother

Ring, ring, ring
7am on the clock
Kids up, get dressed
I'm off to make breakfast
Bacon and eggs
Come on now, we're late once again
Hop in the car, turn on the radio
We are here, off you go
Kids now at school, me now at work
At my desk just to sit there and lurk
3 o'clock
Off to get the kids
Ten minutes pass
I'll just rest for a bit
4pm on the clock
Up again
Doing the laundry and picking up socks
That's all I ask
How can you fail when you only have one task?
6 o'clock
Time to make dinner.
Eat it all
And I'll be a winner
9:30pm on the clock
Get ready for bed

10pm
Time for bed
Get under the blanket
With your stuffed bear Ted
Ring! Ring! Ring!
7:10
Wake up
Here we go again.

Taryn Bowron (12)
Waseley Hills High School, Rubery

You Don't Need To Be Alone To Be Lonely

I flow with the oceans, I flow with the mountains and rivers,
Yet the feeling of isolation is vaster than I can control,
I beg, I plead, "Save me from abandonment,"
You would not survive without my strength, my will,
Yet you only visit me once a year,
Please save me, let me see what they have become,
Corrupting my friends, burning one of them to death,
Greed, envy, power is all they want, never thinking first,
Some try to help. Too small to help. Helpless, he is,
As they rip the sanity from him, I stare, disappointed,
Hope drips away painfully as another one of my friends disappears once again,
You don't need to be alone to be lonely,
Yet I am both.

Holly Eastwood (13)
Waseley Hills High School, Rubery

The Office

There I was in the waiting room for the biggest moment of my life
Would I get the position I wanted?
I've always wanted to be a striker
But they were looking for a left-winger
In every way, my dream would come true
I stepped into the office, adjusted my tie and sat down
I felt like my heart would fly out of my chest
Fortunately, after a long time, I was presented with a contract
'By signing this three-year contract
Your time as a striker for Birmingham City Football Club starts'
Hands shaking, I lifted the pen out of the pot
And wrote my signature, the ink glided across the page
I slid the contract along the marble table
And shook his hand.

Isaac Casey-Jones (13)
Waseley Hills High School, Rubery

Ozzy

I watch my owner laugh and play
I will always love this day
But as the day got weaker, it went so cold and dark
I felt no need to shout or bark
I was safe and warm, snuggling by the fire
It was night, around comes tomorrow
What if there is no tomorrow?
That would be against my desire
What a fright!
I feel the need to sleep tight and right
Watch my owner eye to eye
Sleeping gracefully, like an angel
Just thinking about the play the next day
I love our walks and our talks
Our love, and our sorrow
I'm so excited for tomorrow
But our love is like a dove, beautiful and delicate
I just hope that dove doesn't fly away any time soon.

Jess Atkinson (13)
Waseley Hills High School, Rubery

Untitled

I am a pencil,
My tail tastes of wood,
And my writing is very good,
I can be rubbed out,
But when I make a mistake, people sometimes shout.
Ouch! You can bite me,
But be careful! Because I am feisty,
When you start chewing on me,
I will taste of wood for your tea,
When you write with me,
I will make your work look pretty,
Your work is finished but you made a mistake,
"Ah no, for god's sake,"
I always try my best,
But I don't always impress,
I can be sharpened,
But I always get darkened,
I can be sharp,
But then I always come apart,
Thank you for meeting me,
So until we meet again... owie!

Rose Turner (12)
Waseley Hills High School, Rubery

The Leatherback Turtle

I flap and struggle and cry
For I fear that I shall die.
The nets I am tangled within,
Were left in the ocean by him.
The sailor, with his nets and boats and rods
To lure the fish up,
Though I am not a fish,
I am trapped by what he left behind, the rubbish.
I fight and claw and bite,
To get my leatherback out of it,
But my black fins will never win.
For now, I am struggling, struggling, struggling,
The humans are always hunting, hunting, hunting.
What do they care if I suffer?
What do they care if I die?
They are not affected.
But it affects the animals and I.

Jessica Sharp (12)
Waseley Hills High School, Rubery

My Mistake

I land on the rooftop,
He's there, waiting,
We start fighting and,
I see a news helicopter,
I can overhear, "Batman vs Joker! Who will win?"
They're making entertainment,
Out of war, idiots,
Joker gets a good hit,
Stab in the back,
There's a blur,
I see his sins,
Jason's death,
Barbara.

Then I see that night,
The night I created him,
I see the alley,
Mom, Dad,
No!
Batarang to the shoulder,
A few hits,
He's down,
Were they his sins?
Or mine?
I'm sorry,
Jason, Barbara.

Toby Ross (13)
Waseley Hills High School, Rubery

Blank Page

In my past I breathed the purest air
But that was once before
I'm no longer that tree that stood tall
In the grass
No colours, words or shapes
Either way I couldn't ask
I'm so bland and boring
But I have potential I promise!
But no one can hear me
Hear me
Why won't you hear me?
I lack creativity
I'm just blank
Until
I was chosen
The ink smoothly rolled over me
I was put in a group
Other papers surrounded me
We were stapled together
Agony shot through me
Where am I? Well, I'm the page of this book.

Evie Morgan (13)
Waseley Hills High School, Rubery

Teenager

I force my eyes open and turn off my alarm
I pull myself out of my comfortable bed and look in the mirror
My eyes are almost shut, and underneath them, they are as black as the winter morning sky
The winter air seeps through my window
I get up to brush my teeth and wash my face
As the cold winter hits my face, I wake up
I feel too unmotivated to do anything thoroughly
My stomach growls, and I eat a piece of gum to suffocate its cries
I put on my school uniform and my unlaced shoes that are inappropriate for school
Swinging my bag over my shoulder, I leave my house.

Joseph Kelly (12)
Waseley Hills High School, Rubery

Sacrifice

I have sacrificed the clubs with the flashing lights.
I have sacrificed my body, no more tight dresses that I feel comfortable in.
I have sacrificed my days lying in bed, watching TV.
I am just a mother.

I have sacrificed my time, every hour busy.
I have sacrificed my solitude.
I have sacrificed my privacy, I go nowhere alone.
I am just a mother.

I have sacrificed my whole life for my children.
However, I have gained.
I have gained love with cuddles and kisses at night.
I have gained patience.
I have gained my angels.

Ava Parton (12)
Waseley Hills High School, Rubery

Thinking Weird

Laughter,
Talking,
My brain drifts off to another world,
A dimension,
A rabbit hole, underwater, space, unicorns, aliens, Harry Potter,
Different things going round my head,
Round and round in my head,
My thoughts spinning in my head, spinning like a carousel,
I'm feeling anxious but excited,
I see... things... like...
Giant snakes,
Trolls dancing,
A rabbit in a waistcoat,
A talking caterpillar,
A caterpillar? A caterpillar slithering down a thought in my head,
A shock,
A weird thought,
Weird thoughts?

Juliet Latham (13)
Waseley Hills High School, Rubery

Emily's Pizza

I am cheesy,
Emily likes me done easy,
I'm thick and puffy,
I get cooked till I'm fluffy,
The cheese on my face,
Gets melted at quite the pace,
It isn't a race,
My napkin covers my real face,
When she eats me,
I whisper to her, "Leave me be!"
She ate me anyway,
So in heaven, I rode in a Santa Fe,
Emily ate me so I hate her,
But then I throw up because I am allergic to her,
My journey was long and fun,
Just to end up like Mr Bun,
I am a pizza.

Sophia Seymour-Twist (12)
Waseley Hills High School, Rubery

In My Dreams

In my dreams, my world was perfect
No tears behind my mum's eyes
My sister was as bright as the sun
I was out playing with my friends
But no
In a world of shattered dreams and distant hopes
Through weary eyes, the journey unfolds
Scattered memories of a home left behind
A heart heavy with the weight of the unknown
Faces blur in a sea of unfamiliarity
Through a lens of loss and silent cries
In the search for peace and a place to belong
My eyes reflect the courage to carry on.

Ruby Addis (12)
Waseley Hills High School, Rubery

Crimson Sea

Oh, crimson sea,
Allow me,
Just to take a glance at hope,
Show me greatness,
Dare me to try,
Alas,
The game is now over,
Why?
Nobody can tell me what this is,
Due to the horrid imagery of the subject,
The sun came up above the water,
The blood-drenched bodies that linger in the water,
They drift out,
A funeral, perhaps not?
Surely, there is a way to stop this,
A sign of hope never came,
Nobody escapes from the deadly island of the crimson sea.

Alfred Porter (12)
Waseley Hills High School, Rubery

Deserted

The world has come to a halt,
I've never felt more like an adult,
Loud noises fill the world,
Of sirens, beeps and tears streaming,
Another outbreak is not what I need,
Need to speed to another beep,
Trying to stop people falling asleep,
Struggling to keep them alive,
Whilst the constant buzzing like a bee hive,
I spend my day wishing,
That all this pain will go away,
People trying to thrive,
Whilst they're hidden away inside,
When is it going to stop?

Amelia Turner (13)
Waseley Hills High School, Rubery

Untitled

I sat at the window, watching her walk
She stormed through the door making an angry noise
Their mother approached in an attempt to talk
She shoved her off and slammed her door
I stood up and followed her
And my ears went down at the sight I saw
Saltwater streamed from her eyes
I sat in her arms
Licking her face to calm her cries
She spoke in a language I could not translate
Still I listened to her story
As she said, I was someone she could never hate.

Pepper Pedley (12)
Waseley Hills High School, Rubery

The Fields Of Hell

As I ran,
As we ran,
Everything we knew we were giving up,
One second one life vanished into nothing,
We knew what we were there to do,
What we all had to do,
Guns firing,
Grenades exploding,
Bodies thudded to the floor,
We had only been running for two minutes and all the lives we had lost,
My heartbeat sped,
Sped faster than ever,
My brain told me to stop,
Stop this,
But I couldn't,
I had to fight,
Fight for my country.

Mirren-Rose McMillan (13)
Waseley Hills High School, Rubery

Life Of A Lizard

L ying lazily as the day goes by
I watch the birds as they quickly fly
Z ooming past in groups or by one
A vast feeling of great peace
R esting all day and night
D ozing off without a fright
S omething distracts me despite being at rest

D ay after day even at my best
A lizard's hunger will not stop
Y et being hungry without a halt
S coff plenty I do, so it isn't my fault.

Sam Hallett (13)
Waseley Hills High School, Rubery

In The Air

People coming, people leaving, what I see every day,
Rarely do I ever get a chance to lay,
I fight through the weather day and night,
And some people get a fright,
Sometimes parked, sometimes loose,
I don't always get to choose,
Helping people, young or old,
Always helping them get there when told,
Lifting up, through the clouds,
Seeing the city like a bird,
Dotted across the sky,
A trail would not be shy,
Touching down, everything right,
People will get to their delight.

Nathaniel Matyga (12)
Waseley Hills High School, Rubery

A Day In The Life Of A Hamster – Hammy

Woken up by huge hands
Invading my home. In a box
I shall go. Reaching and
Screeching for help. I wonder how
Long I will have to yelp.
The box moves slowly
I am gripping it with my claws;
A hand scoops me up and
Places me on the floor.
Fresh hay rubs up against my flesh.
Downstairs, I go to my food pot
And grab a yoghurt drop.
In my bed, I dig a hole and go
To sleep. I wonder when I will
Wake again.

Summer Murphy (12)
Waseley Hills High School, Rubery

A Seagull's Day

Swishing through the water
Eating whatever's in sight
Arguing with the other birds
Grabbing strangers' personal belongings
Under benches, I steal
Lurking under bridges
Waiting for my next meal
Over the bright beach
Sun blaring in our sight
Seagulls out of reach
When daytime becomes night
Chips out on the ground
Seagulls fight and play
We fight till one's crowned
Then we become shy.

Maisie-Lea Marsh (12)
Waseley Hills High School, Rubery

WW1

W orking all day, shooting all the Germans until now.
O ver my head fly planes dropping bombs
R ifles shooting all around me
L ying half-dead on the floor, but I keep fighting
D igging my hands into the dirt as I pull myself up

W hile waiting I tried to ignore the pain
A s I shot my gun it launched me back
R ubble falling onto me

1 more year of this.

Julian Kaczorowski (12)
Waseley Hills High School, Rubery

Life Of Pets

D ogs are by far the best pets,
O uch! My paw got trod on,
G rr, it's my boy,
G rr, woof, woof woof,
Y ay, they're home,

I 'm so hungry,
S ausages, we're having sausages,

L ove for all my family,
O h boy, food,
V ipers are so cool,
E veryone's so happy,
D inner is served.

Charlie Ward (12)
Waseley Hills High School, Rubery

Dandelion Field

I am a dandelion, earth's seed spreader,
I am a flower, so bright and well-known,
As rain falls, and wind blows, I spread my seeds and regrow,
My children are around and off goes their adolescence,
People come and go but the predators scare me,
The sloopy ears bounce around and the foxy-red dog runs,
One by one, my kin fall as its claws smush them down,
This is the life of a dandelion.

Reece Roberts (12)
Waseley Hills High School, Rubery

Untitled

The world is gloomy and dark,
I have given up, yet I still feel a surge of hope.
Pitch black, until I see a sudden spark,
Their feet drift away, my heart sinks, I mope.

My home is the streets,
My bed is the drain,
My hair reeks,
Every day is a strain.

I sit with my fellows,
Around the campfire,
The girl next to me bellows,
The chance of survival is dire.

Olivia Lowe (12)
Waseley Hills High School, Rubery

Comet

I'm a spinning, winning, absolutely supersonic comet.
You see me whizzing 'round the globe.
Every move, I plan it.
People see me, and what do they call me?
A shooting star,
A meteor,
An energetic thing,
But still...
I can be relaxed,
Floating through space,
Waiting for my time.
But I am still just,
An absolute live wire,
When it is my time to shine.

Paige Roberts (12)
Waseley Hills High School, Rubery

Hair Bobble Life

I'm a hair bobble. When long things stretch me, it hurts
(I think they're called fingers)
I get really comfortable when I'm in hair
I'm very stretchy
I come in big and small sizes
I am three years old. I don't really know where I came from
I only remember getting taken out of a box
The good thing about me is that I'm very soft, so I am perfect in hair.

Harrison Allsop (12)
Waseley Hills High School, Rubery

Why Am I Like This?

Fatty, ugly
I look in the mirror, why am I like this?
I look in the reflection, why am I like this?
Why can't I be them?
I would rather be them
Why can't I be in a different body?

But then one day I wake up
I'm finally different
But I realise being happy
Is better than being unhappy

So now I pray, stay the same
I am amazing.

Winnie Day (13)
Waseley Hills High School, Rubery

Cat Perspective

Cat lurking looking for food
Prowling in a hungry mood
Always with an attitude

Rat munching out of sight
Eating in the dead of night
Sudden fright, cat bite

Owners open kitchen door
Carcass lying on the floor
Present for you, under paw

Banished to the garden shed
Cat now sleeping on his bed
Tired, now he's fully fed.

Isabella Custance (13)
Waseley Hills High School, Rubery

Strays

I walk on my tired and worn legs
Each step I take is painful
The world around me passes me by
I get nothing more than a kick out of the way
Bad dog, they shout
But how am I different?
The clean and healthy dogs get all the love
While I sleep in the dust and dirt
Maybe one day I'll get the love I deserve
But who could love a stray like me?

Lola McNally (12)
Waseley Hills High School, Rubery

Untitled

At six, I started smoking.
At seven, I was physically abused.
At eight, I never saw my mum again.
At nine, I was tormented by my mum's friend.
This is the story of a former Champions League finalist, Dele Alli.
This is his story. His life.
Being a footballer doesn't take people's sadness away.
Footballers' mental health matters.

Ryan Gillam (13)
Waseley Hills High School, Rubery

Horrifying Reality Of War

In my dreams I think about the WW soldiers,
Stuck in a trench, thinking about their lives and family.
Their best friends that got shot and blown up.
Thinking they were fighting for their country
Worth seeing people that you know die.
Then saying that you're stuck and should fight
Until their last breath and die as a brave hero.

Taha Kamal (13)
Waseley Hills High School, Rubery

A Cat's Day

I woke up in the sun.
Oh, that was very dumb.
So I went inside.
Well, at least I tried.
But I was all out of luck.
A bump on the head,
Could have me lying in bed.
But that's not much like me!
Off I went on a big adventure,
That lasted about two minutes.
Until...
The door flew open and I sprinted there!

Isla Bartlett (12)
Waseley Hills High School, Rubery

Summer And Winter

Feeling the breeze
Hearing the pool
The sky is clear
The sun is near
Ice cream melts
Music is on
I can feel summer
Summer is here

Feeling the freeze
Hearing the chill
The sky is clouded
The snow is near
My brain freezes
Music is off
Silence
I can feel winter
Winter is here.

Amelia Houghton (11)
Waseley Hills High School, Rubery

Perspective

When you think about perspective,
you may think of your loved ones
or even your distant ones
who aren't very friendly.
But what about the animals?
What about the trees?
What about the people who get down on one knee?
Will they say 'yes'?
Will they say 'no'?
Or do I already think that I know?

Jemima Hickman-Smith (11)
Waseley Hills High School, Rubery

The Pigeon

I am a pigeon,
I can fly, walk and bob my head,
When I smell food, I swoop down to reach it,
Humans seem to dislike me,
They say I carry diseases,
But that shouldn't define me,
As I fly, I copy my friends' tricks,
When the sun goes down,
I find my nest,
Once again my friends are beside me.

Kacey Cleaver (12)
Waseley Hills High School, Rubery

Dead Tree

D id you know I am dying?
E very day, I get older,
A ngry men try to cut me down,
D id you know I am still dying?

T reat me like your family,
R espect me, or I'll have my way,
E legant is my word,
E nemies will cut me down but I'll grow back.

Zak Gibbons (12)
Waseley Hills High School, Rubery

I Like Being Rich

The first thing I do when I wake up
Is ask my chef to make breakfast
As I am about to get in my SF90 Ferrari
And go to Farm Foods to get some scran
And get on the highway on my way to my SpaceX Station
And fail some rocket launches
Then go full speed on my 770+hp Koenigsegg
And get a lot of sleep.

Aaron Codinotti (12)
Waseley Hills High School, Rubery

Jordan

Michael Jordan, the basketball star,
From a rich youth, I started very far,
But one scout was all it took,
And it wasn't just luck,
As I stepped onto the NBA court,
I suddenly remember everything I had been taught,
As I peered into the crowd,
I spotted my family,
Their faces very proud.

Sebastian Haywood-Newman (13)
Waseley Hills High School, Rubery

No Meat

V egan burger
E ating meat is bad
G rimace shake
A nimals are alive
N aughty to kill animals

T eaching is good
E at vegan food
A nimals are human
C an you be vegan?
H amburger
E ating vegan
R ats.

Sam McAuliffe (13)
Waseley Hills High School, Rubery

The Place You Stand

I am the shield that protects all
I am the sword that kills
I am the field you harvest
I am your creator
I dance in the night sky
My tears harvested by your machines
The fires you create that fuel my heart
You must care for me, after all, you are adapting
So you can be with me forever.

Kasey Footes (12)
Waseley Hills High School, Rubery

Football

Ouch! Someone's just kicked me and I'm in the air
Wow! There are so many people here
Ow! I see someone's foot
Wet spiky grass is beneath me
Ow! I'm in someone's hands
Ow! I've just been kicked
I'm now in a net of some kind
So many people are here
A whistle blows and the cheering becomes louder.

Alfie Groves (12)
Waseley Hills High School, Rubery

Poppies Everywhere

S truggling to move,
O nly thing to do is run,
L ying down not trying to be seen,
D reaming I was with my family,
I s this ever going to end?
E arth screams for us to stop,
R ed blankets of blood everywhere and the birth of poppy flowers everywhere.

Layla Wheeler (13)
Waseley Hills High School, Rubery

Rivers

R acing down the canal wishing to join the ocean
I n through the forest people hopping over me
V eering from left to right so, so close
E ntering the stream not far now
R aging winds rocking me of course nowhere to go
S uddenly the ocean is there.

Olivia-Mae Brown (11)
Waseley Hills High School, Rubery

Spider

I am a pest,
But I am helpful,
People are scared of me,
While others are not,
You could find me on the spindle,
Next to the sleeping rose,
My hobby is spindling,
I have too many legs to count,
Come with me and I'll trap you in my web,
I am the spider.

Zak Gibbons (12)
Waseley Hills High School, Rubery

I Am Aidan Gallagher

A mazing
I ntelligent
D reamy
A mbitious
N oble

G enerous
A dventurous
L oyal
L oving
A lluring
G lorious
H opeful
E xtravagant
R adiant.

Kasie Rebolo (13)
Waseley Hills High School, Rubery

Lost At War

A gain alone, no one to know and nowhere to go
L onely, locked up like an animal, treated just as bad
O verwhelmed, noise everywhere, battle all around
N o hope lest I'm going to die here
E verything gone in an instant, nothing left.

Dylan Sherwood (12)
Waseley Hills High School, Rubery

Harold's Big Day

My name is Harold Jafar,
I am from afar.
I originate from Qatar.
As I look at my mother,
I say Mashallah to my brother.
Now here I am,
Cuddled in a van,
In the break of dawn,
Recovering from sawn,
As I see Allah,
I shout Alhamdulillah.

Oscar Jabbari (13)
Waseley Hills High School, Rubery

Wheelie Bin

I usually am green
I can be big
Set days are arranged for me to be collected
I get filled up with humans' waste
I have wheels
They are small
I often get dirty
Things rot inside me
What am I?

Answer: I am a wheelie bin!

Hayden Mills (12)
Waseley Hills High School, Rubery

My Hero, Mary Earps

E ngland's first step to success
A gile and powerful, Mary stands above the rest
R ecognised by most, after all she is the best
P retty and presentable, she is well dressed
S tanding above all, she is my favourite Lioness.

Kaitlin Prideaux (12)
Waseley Hills High School, Rubery

Animal

A nd it happened again a bomb in the forest
N o way to escape, no way to be free
I magining a world with peace
M y body in pain being targeted, why?
A nimal, why being one is so hard
L osing everything.

Nicole Pinho (12)
Waseley Hills High School, Rubery

I Was A Noticed Doctor

I was a caregiver
I was a lifesaver
I was a key worker
I was a life provider
I was a truth spitter
I was a puzzle linker
I was an ill finder
I was a time giver
Always remember
I was a noticed doctor.

Jennie-Rose Newey (12)
Waseley Hills High School, Rubery

My Hero

M y hero is Sophie Rain
Y our content motivates me

H elping inspire others
E very day I turn to you
R ising to be just like you
O thers can motivate me but you do it best.

Aiden Fisher (13)
Waseley Hills High School, Rubery

Football

I spend my day practising football,
Wondering if I'll be good enough for a professional football team,
Currently, I am at a Sunday league team for under twelves,
A scout is coming to my game tomorrow and I want to impress.

Bobby Barker (11)
Waseley Hills High School, Rubery

The Burden

The burden
Feeling cold
Smelling like BO
Feeling wet
Smelling of mud
Feeling sticky
Smelling fresh food
Feeling petrified
Smelling seaweed
Feeling rain
I'm a homeless man.

Thomas Mansell (12)
Waseley Hills High School, Rubery

Football Life

I'm a football,
I get punched, kicked and caught,
Sometimes I get fallen on,
But sometimes I get lost,
One day my stitching ripped,
So they put me away on a shelf,
Then I fell and popped.

Charlie Wall (12)
Waseley Hills High School, Rubery

Struggle

Trekking through the forest filled up with grief
Mourning over the loss of a member that I don't want to remember
Still filled with hope for the end
To find a place to rest
It will be the best.

Maximus Ball (11)
Waseley Hills High School, Rubery

Spiders

S taring at you,
P eople feel scared,
I 'm upside down,
D angling from the roof,
E very day,
R unning on your back,
S cared is what you are.

Oscar Larkin (13)
Waseley Hills High School, Rubery

River

Watching the day go by,
Listening silently,
Birds flying from up above,
Leaving hope,

People admiring from afar,
Whilst I watch,
Gently flowing,
Letting everything happen.

Abigail Holden (12)
Waseley Hills High School, Rubery

School Homework

Roses are red,
Violets are blue,
I don't wanna do this,
English is poo.

I'd rather do history,
History is slay,
Geography is boring,
Geography needs to go away.

Lily-May Murren (13)
Waseley Hills High School, Rubery

My First Day

Proud in my new uniform,
Pride all over me,
Happy, excited, joyful,
Nervous and scared,
What if I make no friends?
What if I don't fit in?
What if I get bullied?

Isaac Harley (11)
Waseley Hills High School, Rubery

Through The Eyes Of A Fighter Pilot

Radios echo through the cockpit
As the bad spread, the good perish
Pilots cry as a lot more die
Weapons fire as one loses a tyre
One last breath, then death took the rest.

Harrison Porter (13)
Waseley Hills High School, Rubery

Bin

Hello,
I can be big, I can be small,
You will find me in the kitchen or in a lorry,
I am hated, I cause disgust,
I could never sin,
But, most of all, I am a bin.

Charlie Such (12)
Waseley Hills High School, Rubery

YOUNG WRITERS INFORMATION

We hope you have enjoyed reading this book – and that you will continue to in the coming years.

If you're a young writer who enjoys reading and creative writing, or the parent of an enthusiastic poet or story writer, do visit our website **www.youngwriters.co.uk**. Here you will find free competitions, workshops and games, as well as recommended reads, a poetry glossary and our blog. There's lots to keep budding writers motivated to write!

If you would like to order further copies of this book, or any of our other titles, then please give us a call or order via your online account.

Young Writers
Remus House
Coltsfoot Drive
Peterborough
PE2 9BF
(01733) 890066
info@youngwriters.co.uk

Join in the conversation!
Tips, news, giveaways and much more!